NATIONAL GEOGRAPHIC

READING EXPEDITIONS

SCIENCE SLEUTHS

The Missing Lighthouse

By Glen Phelan

Illustrated by David Opie

PICTURE CREDITS
48 (background) Stacy D. Gold, National Geographic Image Collection; (lower right, inset) © PhotoDisc; (top right, inset) © Georgette Douwma/Getty Images; (center, inset) © Massis J. Boujikian/Corbis

Produced through the worldwide resources of the National Geographic Society, John M. Fahey, Jr., President and Chief Executive Officer; Gilbert M. Grosvenor, Chairman of the Board; Nina D. Hoffman, Executive Vice President and President, Books and Education Publishing Group.

PREPARED BY NATIONAL GEOGRAPHIC SCHOOL PUBLISHING
Ericka Markman, Senior Vice President and President, Children's Books and Education Publishing Group; Steve Mico, Senior Vice President, Publisher, Editorial Director; Francis Downey, Executive Editor; Richard Easby, Editorial Manager; Bea Jackson, Director of Design; Cindy Olson, Art Director; Margaret Sidlosky, Director of Illustrations; Matt Wascavage, Manager of Publishing Services; Lisa Pergolizzi, Sean Philpotts, Production Managers, Ted Tucker, Production Specialist.

MANUFACTURING AND QUALITY CONTROL
Christopher A. Liedel, Chief Financial Officer; Phillip L. Schlosser, Director; Clifton M. Brown, Manager.

EDITORS
Barbara Seeber, Mary Anne Wengel

BOOK DEVELOPMENT
Morrison BookWorks LLC

BOOK DESIGN
Steven Curtis Design

ART DIRECTION
Dan Banks, Project Design Company

Published by the National Geographic Society
1145 17th Street, N.W.
Washington, D.C. 20036-4688

ISBN: 978-0-7922-5829-2

2017 2016 2015 2014 2013
2 3 4 5 6 7 8 9 10 11 12 13 14 15

Printed in Mexico

Contents

Meet the
Science Sleuths

Jamie

Jamie loves drawing and photography. She is a good observer.

Marco

Marco enjoys doing research. He wants to know how things work.

Vanessa

Vanessa is adventurous. She is good at doing science experiments.

Kyle

Kyle likes to interview people. He wants to be a reporter someday.

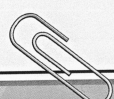

A Curious Message

"**H**ey Jamie, take a look at this," Marco called from the computer.

Jamie looked up from her photographs of wildflowers and walked over to where Marco sat.

A bulletin board hung above the computer. It was loaded with articles, photos, and printouts from Web sites. A sign at the top read:

Science Sleuths:
Tracking Clues, Solving Problems

Among the photos was one of Marco, Jamie, and their friends, Vanessa and Kyle. Together, they were the Science Sleuths.

It was Jamie's idea to start the club. She lived with her Aunt Jessica and Uncle Bill in

Washington, D.C. Aunt Jessica was an editor for a magazine called *National Geographic Explorer!* The magazine covers science stories for students—from bugs to stars and everything in between. Jamie and her friends loved reading it in science class.

Jamie could hardly believe her ears when Aunt Jessica asked if she wanted to help on the magazine. She jumped at the chance—and then realized she needed some help. She asked her friends, Vanessa, Kyle, and Marco, to join her. So began the Science Sleuths.

The Sleuths found answers to questions from readers of *National Geographic Explorer!* They helped Aunt Jessica decide which questions to answer in the magazine. Then they helped her write articles about the questions.

Some of the readers' questions were easy to answer. But some were real puzzlers. And now, from the look on Marco's face, it appeared that another adventure was about to begin.

"What's up?" asked Jamie. She looked over Marco's shoulder at the computer screen.

Marco pointed to the screen. "We got an e-mail about Gull Point Lighthouse. Have you ever heard of it?"

"Gull Point?" came Vanessa's voice from behind. "Sure." She was coming down the stairs with a tray of ham and cheese sandwiches. Kyle was right behind her with a stack of cups and a pitcher of lemonade.

They were at Jamie's house for their official Saturday afternoon meeting. Sometimes the friends spent the day with Aunt Jessica at

National Geographic headquarters in Washington, D.C. But the real Science Sleuths headquarters was a comfortable section of Jamie's basement. There was a small couch and a folding table with chairs. The Sleuths had filled the shelves with all sorts of science books. Everyone's favorite seat was the yellow beanbag chair in the corner. Jamie's framed photos of wildflowers covered the walls.

"It's a really cool lighthouse," continued Vanessa. "It looks like a candy cane."

"Huh?" said Marco.

"You know, it has swirling red and white stripes, like a candy cane," replied Vanessa. She set down the tray of sandwiches and plopped herself into the beanbag chair. "My grandma has a sweatshirt with a bunch of lighthouses on it. That's one of them. What about it?"

"It's missing," said Marco.

"What?" the rest exclaimed together.

"Well, not really missing. But it's not where it used to be. Listen to this." Marco read the e-mail out loud:

Missing Lighthouse

Dear Science Sleuths,

My name is Andrew Paxson. I live in Gull Point, North Carolina, right by the Atlantic Ocean. We have a terrific lighthouse called the Gull Point Lighthouse. It stands on a sand dune by the shore. At least it used to. I have been away on vacation. I just got back. I walked to the lighthouse to check on some seagulls that had built a nest on the ground near it. Guess what? The lighthouse is gone! So is the nest. My mom says they moved the building so that it wouldn't fall into the sea. But why would it suddenly fall into the sea? I don't get it. Can you find out why they moved the lighthouse?

Thanks for your help.
Andrew

"Hmm," said Kyle. "Maybe the lighthouse was so old that it was ready to break apart."

"But how would moving it help?" asked Vanessa. "That would make it fall apart faster."

"Yeah, you're right."

Jamie grabbed one of the sandwiches and said, "Maybe it was starting to lean over, like the Leaning Tower of Pizza."

"That's *Pisa*, not *pizza*," corrected Marco. "Anyway, what would make it lean?"

Kyle poured some lemonade for everyone. "Hey, Marco, why don't you look it up? There must be something about it on the Net."

"I already am," said Marco. He finished typing *Gull Point Lighthouse* in the search field on the computer and hit *ENTER*. Several entries came up. He opened one and read through it. "Yep, it was moved all right. It says here that they moved it a thousand feet over ten days."

"Let's see," said Vanessa. "1,000 divided by 10 equals 100. Wow, only a hundred feet a day. That's slow. I can crawl faster than that."

Marco continued. "It says the lighthouse was put on a platform with wheels. It crept slowly and had to stop a lot along the way."

"Does the article say why they had to move it?" asked Kyle.

Marco read aloud. "The move was necessary because of continued beach erosion. Several attempts were made to save the Gull Point Lighthouse over the last ten years, but nothing worked. Engineers concluded that if the lighthouse were left where it was, it would be in danger of falling into the sea in just a few years."

"So the article says the problem is **erosion,** right?" said Kyle. "Didn't we learn something about that in science class last year?"

"Sure," said Jamie. "Erosion happens when wind, ice, or water moves soil and pieces of rock."

"Like a river," added Marco. "The moving water flows along the riverbank and takes bits of soil with it as it moves." He held out one hand, keeping it still, as he swiped his other hand against it like water rushing fast against a riverbank. *"Whooosh!"*

"The water pushes pebbles along the bottom of the river, too," said Vanessa. "So the river carries away soil and rock bit by bit."

---

erosion - the moving of loose rock and soil to another place

"Don't forget the wind," said Kyle. "Wind blows grains of sand into big sand dunes in the desert and on the beach."

"But how would erosion at the beach make a lighthouse fall down?" asked Jamie.

Vanessa thought for a moment. "I have an idea for an experiment that might help us figure it out. C'mon, we have to go outside." She jumped up out of the beanbag chair.

"Wait a second," insisted Marco. "I want to finish looking through these articles."

"Okay, but hurry up," urged Vanessa. Sometimes she got impatient when there were experiments to do. She knew that reading and research were important. She just preferred to do science rather than read about it. Marco, on the other hand, loved reading about and researching all sorts of things. He was also a whiz at searching the Internet.

Marco opened the other articles one by one and skimmed through them. Kyle peered over his shoulder. "Can you find anything about how they tried to save the lighthouse before they moved it?" Kyle asked.

"Nope, doesn't look like it," replied Marco.

Kyle thought out loud, "Hmm, I wonder if I could talk to someone to find out."

The Sleuths were definitely getting interested in the moving lighthouse. "Looks like a good question to explore," said Jamie. "Why don't you e-mail Andrew and tell him that we're on the case? But first let's finish lunch."

On the Trail

With the last sandwich eaten, the Sleuths rushed outside into Jamie's backyard. It was a beautiful day in late June. The bright, warm sunshine felt good.

"I'll race you to the sandbox," Vanessa called. She took off with a good head start, but Kyle caught up quickly and beat everyone. He usually did. He was a terrific athlete and faster than most kids his age.

The sandbox was in the shape of a turtle. Jamie hadn't played in it for a couple of years, but her aunt and uncle hadn't gotten around to getting rid of it yet. The lid was the turtle's shell. Vanessa slid the lid off and knelt down in the grass. "C'mon, help me move all this sand over." Everyone knelt down and started pushing all the sand to one side. The bottom showed where the sand was scraped away.

"Good. Now let's get the hose," said Vanessa. Marco picked up the end of the water hose. It was stretched out in the grass.

"I'll turn it on," called Kyle as he ran toward the faucet on the side of the house.

"I'm going to run and grab my sketchbook," said Jamie.

While she went into the house, Marco filled the empty side of the sandbox with water.

"About halfway should do it," said Vanessa.

Jamie came running up with her sketchbook and pencil in hand.

"Okay," said Vanessa. "The sand is the sandy beach and the water is the ocean. And here come the waves." She swept her hand through the water to make waves. Each wave hit the beach straight on.

Jamie was the first to notice what was happening. "Look! See how the sand moves?" As each wave lapped against the sand, the water moved some sand grains.

"I don't see it," said Kyle.

Jamie pointed to the sand. "Each wave pushes

sand grains up the shore. Then the grains move back down a little toward the water."

"Oh, yeah," said Kyle. "Let me try."

Each took turns making waves. They could all now see how the shape of the "beach" was changing before their eyes. "So the waves wear away the beach sand. That's what beach erosion is," proclaimed Vanessa.

After a few minutes, a big clump of sand slid into the water. "Oh, cooool," Kyle said.

Kyle looked around and grabbed a small twig. He stuck it into the sand near the water's edge. "That's the lighthouse," he said.

In just a few minutes, the waves washed away the sand at the base of the twig. It started to lean. "There it goes!" called Marco. The twig toppled into the water. "And that's what was going to happen to the Gull Point Lighthouse," he concluded.

Jamie made a few quick drawings to show how the water eroded the sand around the twig.

"Hey, kids, what are you up to?" Aunt Jessica asked as she walked up to them.

"Hi, Aunt Jess," Jamie said.

"Hi, Mrs. Cooper," said the rest of the Sleuths.

"I knew if we kept this sandbox you'd put it to good use," Aunt Jessica said with a big smile. "So are you playing or investigating?"

Jamie told her about the e-mail from Andrew, their experiment, and what they had found out so far about the Gull Point Lighthouse.

"You know, your uncle and I took a trip to Gull Point about 10 years ago. It's a beautiful place. And the lighthouse is really old. I think there was talk back then about somehow trying to save it."

"What were they going to do?" asked Kyle.

"I don't know. I just remember they were going to have a town meeting to discuss it."

"Well, whatever they tried, I guess it didn't work," said Vanessa.

"I'd sure like to find out what happened," said Kyle.

"So would our reader Andrew Paxson," added Aunt Jessica. "In fact, I'll bet a lot of our readers would. How about if we **investigate** this question for the magazine? We could find out how they tried to save the lighthouse and write an article about it."

Everyone thought that was a good idea. Then Jamie said, "Boy, I'd sure love to see that lighthouse." The Sleuths all nodded in agreement.

----

investigate - to observe, study, or examine

"You know what?" said Aunt Jessica. "I wouldn't mind seeing it again myself." She had that smile on her face that Jamie knew well.

"Do you think we can take a trip?" Jamie asked hopefully.

"Sure. I'm on vacation for a few days. And what better way to investigate erosion than to see it in action? We could leave tomorrow and come back Wednesday. I'll call your folks and make sure it's okay with them. Does that sound like a plan?" The high fives gave her the answer.

Chapter 3

A Trip to the Shore

The next day, just before eight o'clock, Aunt Jessica honked the horn outside Kyle's house. Backpack on, Kyle appeared with his mom. She tried to brush his hair and give him a kiss, but he ducked out of the way.

"Mom, not in front of the guys," he groaned. "Bye. See you in a couple days."

"Hi, guys. Hi, Mrs. C." He jumped in and buckled his seatbelt. Everyone else was on board.

"And we're off," announced Aunt Jessica.

Marco was sitting in the front seat. He was the navigator. He had the map unfolded about halfway so that he could see their entire route. Marco turned in his seat and showed the map to his friends. They were sitting together in the middle seat of Aunt Jessica's minivan. "Here's where we are," he said, pointing to Washington, D.C., "and here's where we're going." He moved his finger south on the map and ended at the coast of North Carolina.

"Hey, it's an island!" said a surprised Vanessa.

"That's right," said Aunt Jessica to the kids. "It's a barrier island."

"What's that?" asked Jamie.

"Well, do you know what a barrier is?" Aunt Jessica prodded. The Science Sleuths were used to Aunt Jessica not giving an answer right away. It was the science teacher in her. She was a teacher for several years before working for National Geographic. She tried to get kids to figure things out for themselves.

Vanessa thought for a few seconds. "A barrier is something that blocks something else."

"Oh, I get it," said Marco. "Look at the map. There's a whole string of long, skinny islands that go up and down the coast. Those islands probably block the mainland from the strongest winds and biggest ocean waves. Right?"

Aunt Jessica smiled and nodded.

Jamie thought more about it. "That means the barrier islands must really take a pounding."

Kyle shook his head slightly. "I don't know. It's still hard to believe that erosion could make the lighthouse fall. I mean, it's a big, strong building."

"But think of our experiment," said Vanessa.

"I know, I know," said Kyle. "But a lighthouse isn't a twig. It's just hard to imagine."

"Well you don't have to imagine it," said Aunt Jessica. "Erosion is all around you. In fact, here's some erosion right now." She pointed out the window. "See that hill over there?" They were passing a construction site where there was a huge pile of sand and gravel. It was as tall as a five-story building. There were deep **gullies,** or little valleys, that ran down the hill on all sides.

"They built that hill last year when they started digging up the ground. It looked like a big, smooth gumdrop. Look how it's changed."

"How did erosion do that?" asked Kyle.

"Rain," said Aunt Jessica.

"Really?"

----
gully - a small valley caused by running water

"Sure," said Aunt Jessica. "It's amazing how moving water shapes the land."

The Science Sleuths thought about that for a few minutes. Then they talked about other things, such as movies, music, and sports. Kyle and Vanessa took turns playing a video game. Marco was looking at the map, imagining that he was on a boat exploring the coast. Jamie had her headphones on. She was drawing pictures of lighthouses in her sketchbook.

The rest of the trip was quiet—until the ocean came into view. Then everyone perked up again. They crossed over a long bridge that connected the mainland to the island. A half hour later, they pulled up to the Sunrise Motel.

The motel was near the ocean. A cool sea breeze greeted the travelers as they piled out of the van. "I can taste the salt in the air," said Jamie. Seagulls glided overhead and called to one another. The steady waves breaking on shore made a soothing sound. The deep blue water sparkled in the sunshine.

"It's just like I remember it," said Aunt Jessica, looking around. "Okay, let's get our gear inside." They unpacked and settled into their rooms. Kyle and Marco shared a room. Aunt Jessica was with the girls next door.

It was late afternoon. The first order of business was to see the lighthouse. They didn't have to ask for directions. Brand-new signs pointed the way to Gull Point Lighthouse. The motel clerk said that the town was having a ceremony on Wednesday to celebrate the new location. People were coming in from all over. Even the governor was going to speak.

Aunt Jessica and the Sleuths followed the signs down Main Street. They walked up a side street, through a grassy area, and up a little hill. Another turn, a slight rise, then . . ."There it is!" Kyle yelled.

"Hey, Vanessa, it really does look like a candy cane," said Jamie.

The red and white stripes of Gull Point Lighthouse gleamed in the sunshine. The building was more than a hundred feet tall.

Jamie took a picture of the lighthouse with her new digital camera. A few people were just coming out of the lighthouse door. "Thanks for visiting, folks," said a guide who stood outside. He turned to the Sleuths. "Would you like to go up? It's a terrific view."

"Can we? Please, Aunt Jess?" Jamie asked, pleading.

"Sure. But let's be careful up there by that railing."

Inside, a narrow staircase wound all the way up to the top. Everyone had to climb in single file. "Boy, you can get dizzy doing this," observed Marco. A few small windows lit the way.

It took five minutes to reach the top. They stepped through a door and out onto the walkway that circled the tower. "Wow, what a view!" exclaimed Kyle. They could see for miles. Everyone was pointing

out different things: a boat way out in the water, a sandy point that jutted out into the ocean.

Vanessa noticed the waves. "Look at how the waves come in to shore. They hit the beach on a slant. They don't hit the shore straight on like the waves we made in the sandbox. I wonder why."

Jamie was snapping pictures. Suddenly she stopped. "Hey, there's where the lighthouse used to be! Do you see it?"

She pointed to a sandy path that led through a clump of trees. The path was as wide as a road. They could see tracks in the sand. They were made by the wheels of the platform that moved the lighthouse. The path ended at a slab made of old concrete.

"That must be the old **foundation** of the lighthouse," observed Aunt Jessica.

"Boy, look how close the waves come," said Marco. As each wave broke onshore, the water came rushing up to the edge of the foundation. "During storms, the waves must have been splashing right against the lighthouse."

A few seagulls circled above the foundation. Then one landed on the edge of it. That made everyone remember Andrew's e-mail. In it, he had mentioned the seagulls that nested there. "I hope they find another home," said Vanessa.

"Okay, kids, let's head down so that others can come up," Aunt Jessica said. "Besides, it's time for dinner. Who's hungry?"

---

foundation - the base or support of a structure or building

A Changing Shoreline

"Marco, Kyle, are you up?" Vanessa was knocking on the door to the boys' room. It sounded more like pounding to Kyle.

"Yeah, yeah, I'm up," Kyle groaned. Marco was brushing his teeth. But Kyle was still lying in bed, buried in his pillows.

Vanessa's job was to get the boys "up and at 'em," as Aunt Jessica liked to say. "C'mon, there's lots to do. We have to eat breakfast, check out the newspaper office, go to the . . ." WHUMP! She jumped back as a pillow hit the other side of the door. Kyle wasn't exactly a morning person.

After breakfast, they all went to the offices of the *Gull Point Gazette.* It was a busy office. The receptionist said that several reporters from other newspapers were in town for the lighthouse ceremony. They were at the *Gazette* office to get background information for their articles.

"That's why we're here, too," said Kyle.

"Really?" asked the receptionist. She seemed impressed. That made Kyle and the Sleuths feel proud.

"Yes, ma'am," Kyle said politely. "We're reporters for *National Geographic Explorer!* magazine. We'd like to find out how they tried to save the lighthouse before they had to move it. Can you help us?"

"Well, we have some information in our files about it, but the other reporters are going through them now. Why don't you talk to Mike? He works with the Army Corps of Engineers. They were in charge of saving the lighthouse and moving it."

"Terrific!" exclaimed Kyle.

"His office is set up in a trailer at the end of the parking lot by the public beach."

They thanked the receptionist for her help and left the newspaper office. The Sleuths and Aunt Jessica made their way across the parking lot to the trailer.

"Come in," called a voice from inside.

They found Mike Amato looking over some

blueprints that were unrolled on a large slanted table. He looked up and smiled at his visitors. "Good morning, folks. What can I do for you?"

This time, Vanessa explained who they were and what they hoped to find out. Mike said he was happy to talk to them. "In fact," he said, "I have some photos that will be very helpful."

Jamie perked up at the mention of photos.

"Let's see, where did I put those things? Oh, yes, here they are." Mike pulled a large yellow envelope from a filing cabinet. He rolled up the blueprints and set them aside. Then he pulled out a pile of photographs from the envelope and set the pile neatly on the table. Everyone gathered around. They could see that the photos were taken from the air.

Kyle had his notebook out, ready to take notes. Mike noticed and nodded his approval.

"First, a little background," he said. "The Gull Point Lighthouse was built in 1875."

"Wow, that's a long time ago. I didn't realize that it was so old," said Jamie.

"Yes," said Mike. "And here's something else I

bet you didn't know. When the lighthouse was built, it was a thousand feet from shore."

"Really?" said Jamie. The Sleuths were shocked. Even Aunt Jessica looked surprised.

"Yep," said Mike. "That's how much the shoreline changes on these barrier islands. Erosion is constantly washing away the sand from one place and dropping it someplace else."

"By about ten years ago, so much beach had eroded that the lighthouse was only a hundred feet from the water. Something had to be done fast. So we built these jetties." He pointed to two objects in the photo on top of the pile. "Jetties are low walls that go from the shore out into the water. They went out about five hundred feet."

"Did people build the jetties to trap sand and keep it from washing away?" asked Jamie.

"Good observation, Jamie. Yes, the jetties did what they were supposed to do. You see, waves strike the beach at a slant, or an angle. That moves the sand along the beach."

"Just like what we saw yesterday from the lighthouse," said Vanessa. She explained to Mike how they noticed the waves hitting the beach at a slant instead of straight on.

"That's right, Vanessa. The waves were moving the sand along the beach. But that's only one way the water moves the sand. The sand also moves because of something called a longshore current."

The Sleuths looked puzzled.

"A current is like a river of water flowing through the ocean."

That didn't help.

Mike thought a moment. "Did you ever make a whirlpool in a tub by swirling your hand through the water? A current is like a whirlpool that's stretched out into a fairly straight line.

"A longshore current moves along the shoreline just a little bit away from the shore. Together, the waves and longshore currents move large amounts of sand each year. The jetties trapped some of this sand in front of the lighthouse. That built up the beach by the lighthouse, which is what we wanted. But do you know what problems the jetties caused?"

Aunt Jessica smiled. Mike was being a very good teacher.

"Look on the other side of the jetties," Mike said, pointing to the photo.

"Oh, I see it," said Marco. "There's only a little sand on the other sides of the jetties."

"Right," added Jamie. "The jetties stopped sand from moving to other parts of the shoreline."

"Exactly," said Mike. "The sand trapped by the jetties would have normally replaced the eroded sand farther along the shore. Beaches to the south lost too much sand. So we took out

some of the jetties." Then Mike placed the next two photos side by side.

"Next, we tried something called beach nourishment. That simply means adding sand to the beach to build it up."

"Where do you get the sand?" asked Kyle.

"Different places. For Gull Point, we got it from big sand dunes on the mainland. We brought sand in by the truckload. You can see the difference before and after we added sand."

The photos clearly showed a wider beach after the sand was added.

"The problem is, it's very expensive to haul sand. In order to keep up with erosion, we'd have to haul a couple of times a year. There had to be a better way."

"Couldn't you just build a wall around the lighthouse?" asked Marco.

"Good point, Marco. We thought about doing that. But erosion would continue around the wall. Then the lighthouse would become an island. We didn't want that. So the best solution was to move it back. We placed it on higher ground, which is good."

"Is it safe now?" asked Jamie.

"For at least a hundred years. It will never be

totally safe. Erosion continues."

"Speaking of erosion," said Vanessa, "could we explore the shore now, Mrs. C?"

"Sure. We shouldn't take up any more of Mike's time anyway. Thanks so much for all your help."

"Yes, thank you," they all said as they shook Mike's hand.

"My pleasure. When your article comes out, send me a copy, will you?"

They promised they would. Jamie asked Mike if they could use the photos for the article. "No problem," he said. He would e-mail them information about how to get copies.

Out on the beach, the Sleuths kicked off their shoes and rolled up their pants to wade in the surf. The water was cold on their toes. Marco, Jamie, and Aunt Jessica were happy just to get their feet wet. But Vanessa and Kyle went in above their ankles.

"Whoa!" called Vanessa. "Do you feel that?"

Even though they were in only a few inches of water, the rushing waves nearly knocked them off their feet. And the water that washed back toward the ocean nearly pulled them in. It was an awesome power.

"Imagine what waves many feet high can do, especially during a storm," Aunt Jessica said.

Seagulls kept the Sleuths company as they waded along the shore. Jamie thought about Andrew Paxson, who had e-mailed them. "Hey, guys! Why don't we look up Andrew and let him know what we found out?" They all agreed to do that the next day.

Case Closed

The Science Sleuths spent the next day having some fun. They found Andrew Paxson's address in the phone book and dropped by for a visit. He and his parents were thrilled. The Paxsons invited them all to stay for lunch and then everyone went to the beach together.

The Sleuths and Andrew built an amazing sand castle. It was more like a sand town, at least until some waves came ashore and turned it into a sand pond. But that was okay. It gave them a close-up view of erosion at work.

The next day, the Sleuths made one last stop at the lighthouse before their trip home. They stared up at the candy cane tower.

"I bet it's seen a lot of storms since 1875," said Kyle.

"And saved a lot of ships from running into the shore at night," said Vanessa.

Aunt Jessica used Jamie's camera to take one last picture of the four friends near the lighthouse. As they stood there posing, Jamie heard a soft purring sound, like a pigeon.

"Shhh. Listen," she said.

The others heard it, too. They carefully walked around the lighthouse. After walking about ten feet, they stopped. So did the purring. Then they saw it. In a clump of grass, up against the brick tower, a seagull had made a nest. Was

it the same gull that Andrew had seen by the shore? They hoped so. And now they all knew how they were going to end their article about moving Gull Point Lighthouse.

When the Sleuths returned back home, they helped Aunt Jessica put the article together for *National Geographic Explorer!*

They worked as a team. Marco gathered more research from the Internet about other lighthouses that had been moved. He also found information about the huge platform that slowly carried the lighthouse to its new home.

Kyle reviewed his notes from the interview with Mike. Then he wrote the interview clearly.

Vanessa wrote notes about the experiment they did in the sandbox. Then she compared the experiment with what they saw at the beach.

Finally, Jamie loaded her pictures into the computer. Then everyone gathered around to pick a few pictures that told the story best. They could only pick two because they wanted to leave room for at least one picture that Mike showed them. So they chose one that showed the waves hitting the old lighthouse foundation. Then they picked the one of the four of them in front of the lighthouse.

Aunt Jessica thought it was a good choice—and another success for the Science Sleuths.

What Is Erosion?

Erosion is the process of moving material from one place to another. There are several causes of erosion in nature. Four of them are: water, ice, wind, and gravity.

Water Erosion Rushing water is powerful. It can carry away soil and rock. Waves on a beach can sweep away sand and carry it to other places.

Ice Erosion A glacier is a huge body of ice that slowly moves over land. When a glacier slides over rocks, it scrapes them and breaks them apart. The glacier then moves these rock pieces as it flows downhill.

Wind Erosion The wind can create hills of sand called dunes. Dry sand is picked up by the wind. The wind then piles the sand up to form a dune. Sand dunes can be found on some ocean beaches. The wind blows from the ocean. It picks up sand and piles it up farther back on the beach.

Gravity Erosion Gravity moves rocks and soil from a high place to a low place. If rocks become loosened, gravity can cause them to roll down to lower ground. Sometimes buildings can be destroyed when rock and soil move downhill. This type of gravity erosion is called a landslide.

Be a Science Sleuth

The Science Sleuths used their questioning and research skills to solve a science mystery. Now you can be a sleuth, too.

- Copy the web below into your notebook.
- Choose a type of erosion and write it in the center oval.
- Fill the other ovals with questions you would like to research.
- Use books and the Internet to find answers to your questions.
- Write a three-paragraph essay explaining what you have learned from your research.

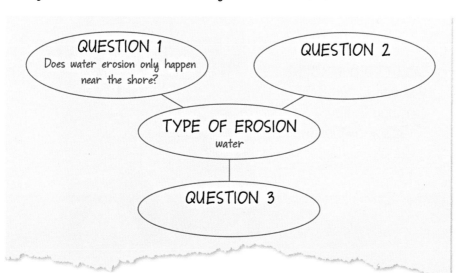

QUESTION 1
Does water erosion only happen near the shore?

QUESTION 2

TYPE OF EROSION
water

QUESTION 3

Read More About Erosion

Find and read more books about erosion. As you read, think about these questions. They will help you understand more about this topic.

- What are the different types of erosion?
- Which types of erosion occur where you live?
- How does Earth's surface change as a result of erosion?
- How can erosion impact people's lives?
- How do people try to prevent erosion?

SUGGESTED READING
Reading Expeditions
Everyday Science:
Science at the Sandy Shore